There It Is

Ashton Liston

Presentation by *BookLeaf Publishing*

Web: www.bookleafpub.com

E-mail: info@bookleafpub.com

ISBN: 9789357696272

First edition 2023

DEDICATION

To my sister,

For all the gentle nudges

who is this man?

yesterday belongs
to a straw-haired
momma's boy, scared
and prone to tears

today he asks
who is this man?

cold-skinned and careful
behind thin
steamed glasses, asleep
through golden years

but still he asks
who is this man?

before he was a headstone
but after he fell
I'm love, so deep
his ears are still wet

too afraid to ask
who is this man?

he bears no cross
upon his "never
look backs", hoping
they won't forget

why he still asks
who is this man?

one extra screw

If I could think straight right now,
I would write about something
that would move you.
Like I used to.

I could deconstruct
a structureless life,
and when I put it back
together
there would be one extra screw.

I would twist phrases
into knots so tight
that when my graceless fingers
finally get them
undone
they will mean nothing.

I could come clean
and leave cleaner
and come back
with a boxful of
something to believe in
but it will be empty

I would but I am paranoid, or
at least predisposed
to get under the skin
of some profoundly
pointless questions.
to gnaw on them like bones.

Sugar and Coffee

Smother me with love,
Scoop up my last breath into
Your China glass hands

Carry it away
To your backseat and let it
Linger on your clothes

Sour lips, cyanide
Seven dollar bills and your
Third busted tail light

Can you count the ways
People count their endless days,
Scavengers of time

Seven million years
Pass in fog on the windows,
And we are alone

Fragile leads fragile
Brokenness binds together,
Sugar and Coffee

Infinite Waves

Last night the sky melted
Forever long strings of
Galactic spit and spent fumes.
And when the morning came,
(Though by then we called it grief)
We watched with tear speckled cheeks
The children splashing in sporadic
Celestial puddles
Until they were soaked and sporting
Angel wings

Come afternoon
Trees fell, hurried,
Swept into a milky current
Streets flooded
Til only dirty leather hands
Could reach above
Infinite waves
But found nothing
To hold on to

When evening fell,
Cities swallowed
In deep star oceans,
Few remained in monasteries

And cathedrals
And 4-Star hotel rooms,
And all that could be heard was
The steady drip
Of eternal pour

The more devout among us
Believed it was rapture
The more religious prayed it was not
And I myself
Plagued by that perpetual
And ineffable indecision,
Resigned to consummation

cigarette smoke

tonight
i think of love as
a quiet cloud of
cigarette smoke sneaks in
through my
bedroom window.

when i say i love you
to my friend
it means my voice on
the other end of the phone
when the shadows from your head
are now dancing on your walls,
and i will talk you through
the revelation that fear and awe
are not far off.
it means i will accept
the weight you throw onto my shoulders, gladly,
when it gets too much to bear.

when i say i love you
to my family
it means mountains
and oceans and
existential planes
cannot separate us.
it means state lines

may exist on maps,
but my love will cross boldy,
any border.
it means you are my home.

when i say i love you to her
it means being buried alive
underneath layers of
frantic heartbeats,
bedsheets,
and a love that transcends love
and becomes one single
shared breath
inhaling late night epiphanies
and coughing out
paper hearts.

i love you in very much
the same way the stars shine for the earth, the way the
oceans gently kiss the shore

the way smoke sneaks in through a bedroom window

A Man Walks Into A Bar

A man walks into a bar...
Stop me if you've heard this one before.
A man walks into a bar,
the same bar every night.
The same seat,
the same drink,
The same friend by his side.
Swallows his fear and chases with beer
and fumbles with the question:
"Why are we here?"
His friend snorts and he spits
and he laughs and he chokes.
The man says,
"What if my life was merely a joke?"

relics

i
look
at five
christmas
tree ornaments
she made sure i had
with me when i moved.
i see a dusty shrine and a quiet
reminder i will no longer hang from her tree
and I
don't
know
where to put them

The Flower Still Grows

When you're up to your neck in the tears you have cried
And you offer your envy to those who have died
And accept that your truths will be taken as lies
You haven't got time to look back.
The children can see but we choose to be blind
And the flower still grows from the sidewalk crack

Now the ones that protect us are turning away
And a powerful people are turning to prey
The reaper has come and we've asked him to stay
We can use him when we attack
The battle will rage and the warriors will pray
That the flower still grows from the sidewalk crack

And they usher our souls through industrial farms
Led by the grasp of invisible arms
But they pay us real good while they're doing us harm
In their favor, the odds always stacked
You can blow all the whistles and sound the alarms
But the flower still grows from the sidewalk crack

So rush now to the booths, make heard your voice
Pencil in your favorite illusion of choice
Both sides saying nothing, commercialized noise
Shades of grey, not white and black
The machine keeps on humming and the cogs they rejoice
And the flower still grows from the sidewalk crack

So the end of an era greets a new one again
And the old and the young must soon become friends
One versed in the past, one staring ahead
It's time to pick up the slack
If we don't come together, then we come to an end
But the flower still grows from the sidewalk crack

Branches

Sane spirit
in strange body.
Cannot remember
the way the tree looked
when it's branches
were still covered
with leaves

Tracks

Like footprints in the snow
Cemented in our impermanence
Afraid of warmer weather
But cannot bare the cold

Aging Like an Apple

We all must pay our dues regardless,
of the cost
where will you go when your,
paradise is lost?
Will you remember what he whispered,
absolute?
Baby teeth sinking into ripe flesh,
The sweetness of the fruit

"We all must leave the garden someday"

One Hand Clapping

I've asked the sages
To pour over the pages
Of koans she'd sewed on to me
But the sages took ages
And I spent all my wages
On the poor sages hospital fees

Tick Tick

I look at a mess
and I see I am afraid of change

10,000 hours spent ignoring
and watching reruns

Slipping into the same clothes
piled up and tired

Feeding lines to familiar ears
for some semblance of reason

Made of cold stone and jealousy
and faltering truths

I Am

I am floating in the deep end
I am soaring through the trees
I am a feather on the breeze
And I am the breeze
I am

I am swimming in the water
I am crawling upon the land
I am buried head first in the sand
And I am the sand
I am

I am laughing in the darkness
Yes I am rolling in my grave
I am performing on the stage
And I am the stage
I am

I am shining through the window
I am resting in my cave
I am falling on my blade
And I am the blade
I am

I am bathing in the moonlight
I am standing by the wall
I am sipping on the stars
And i am the stars
I am

I am lying on the river
I am curving around the bend
I am coming to an end
And I am the end
I am

I am just a drop of water
No I am the ocean, every wave
I am just a single second
No I am a lifetime, every day

I am the hands that build and blunder
I am the waves that carry sound
I am the bellowing of thunder
I am emerging from the ground

Yes I am moving, and I am running
And I am simple, and I am stunning
And I am quiet and I am proud
And I am humble and I am loud
And I am belief and I am belived
And I am deception, I am deceived
I am conception being conceived
And I am perception being perceived

I am climbing up the mountain
I am standing at the peak
I am cultivating poetry
And I am the poetry
And I am the poetry
And I am

Afternoon

Wandering around this town
for hours now and now I've found
that hours pass without you faster,
weeps my broken telecaster

God disguised as Holy Bible
Come deny the idol vinyl
Vital signs hang in the balance
Forgery or is it talent?

Hum of quiet conversation
Pause for humble explanation
There's a place inside your head
that echoes all the things you said

Time has come for retribution
Which is truth and which illusion?
Some confusion has no answer,
Weeps my broken telecaster

Maybe, Maybe Not

Good and bad divide
Eternity spirals out
Only truth is left

There It Is

You will find nothing here.

I am a balloon in the slippery hand of
a child standing idle on the boardwalk
and in seconds or years I will be released
into the grey sky

And for a while I will fly there
Hell, I may even die there

But for now I'm lying in the darkness
letting the summer ants crawl on my skin
and in the s p a c e s between sad songs
i ask them their opinions

and they tell me
You will find nothing here.

Son of a Fatherless Man

I was born yellow
and weeping
in the wake
of fresh grief

Plucked into a tank
and bathed in light
and they covered
my eyes

I was born fearful
and boasted
in the face
of an unworn pain

Lifted to the sky
and baptized
when I opened
my eyes

I was born watchful
and patient,
the silver-lining in a funeral suit
the son of a fatherless man

www.ingramcontent.com/pod-product-compliance
Lightning Source LLC
LaVergne TN
LVHW021354200726

843509LV00014B/2838